Fighting men of Highland Catholic Jacobite Clan who Fought in Canada to Gain it for, and Preserve it to, the Crown, and for the Honour of the Name of Glengarry

Macdonell of Glengarry

FIGHTING MEN

of a

HIGHLAND CATHOLIC
JACOBITE CLAN WHO
FOUGHT IN CANADA
TO GAIN IT FOR AND
PRESERVE IT TO

The Crown

AND FOR THE HONOUR
OF THE NAME OF

Glengarry

Macdonell of Glengarry

FIGHTING MEN

of a

HIGHLAND CATHOLIC
JACOBITE CLAN WHO
FOUGHT IN CANADA
TO GAIN IT FOR AND
PRESERVE IT TO

The Crown

AND FOR THE HONOUR
OF THE NAME OF

Glengarry

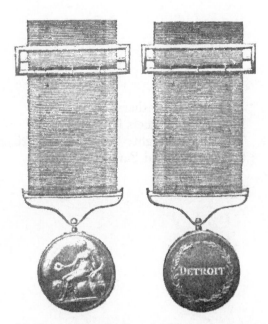

Obverse of Gold Medal awarded to Lieut.-Col. John Macdonell (Red George
for Ogdensburg and Chateauguay.   Reverse of Gold Medal awarded
to Lieut.-Col. John Macdonell, P.A.D.C., to commemorate
the capture of Detroit.

"Fight as your fathers fought,
  Fall as your fathers fell;
  Thy task is taught; thy shroud is wrought—
So, Forward and Farewell!"

—*Praed.*

"I sought for merit wherever it could be found. It is my boast that I was the first Minister who looked for it and found it in the Mountains of the North. I called it forth and drew into your service a hardy and intrepid race of men; men who, left by your jealousy, became a prey to the artifices of your enemies, and had gone nigh to have overturned the State in the War before last. These men in the last War were brought to combat on your side; they served with fidelity, as they fought with valour, and conquered for you in every quarter of the world."

—*The Earl of Chatham*, 1776.

CONQUEST OF CANADA.

Note—The names mentioned in the following lists are only of those who held Commissions in the various Regiments   It would be practically impossible, at this late date, to compile a full and accurate list of the Non-Commissioned Officers and men , it may be safely assumed, however, that they were about in proportion to the Commissioned Officers, practically every man of the name, whatever his rank or station in life, being a fighting man when occasion required.

CONQUEST OF CANADA.

Taking of Louisburg, 1758.

Taking of Quebec.

Battle of the Heights of Abraham, 1759.

1. John Macdonell (Lochgarry)—Captain 78th Regiment (Fraser's Highlanders); afterwards Colonel 76th Regiment (Macdonald Highlanders); wounded at the taking of Quebec. (Had previously served in the Garde Ecossaise, Ogilvie's Corps, after Culloden. The attainder was levied in his favour.)

2. Charles Macdonell, son of Glengarry—Captain 78th Regiment (Fraser's Highlanders); wounded at the Battle of the Heights of Abraham; killed at the capture of St. John's, Newfoundland.

3. Ranald Macdonell, son of Keppoch—Lieutenant 78th Regiment (Fraser's Highlanders); wounded at the taking of Quebec.

4. William Macdonell — Lieutenant 78th Regiment (Fraser's Highlanders).

5. John Macdonell (Leek)—Lieutenant 78th Regiment (Fraser's Highlanders); wounded at the taking of Louisburg; served through the Revolutionary War; died a Colonel in the service. (He had been on the staff of Prince Charles Stuart in 1745, and was twice wounded at Culloden.)

6. Alexander Macdonell (son of Barrisdale)—Lieutenant 78th Regiment (Fraser's Highlanders); killed at the taking of Quebec.

REVOLUTIONARY WAR.

REVOLUTIONARY WAR.

1776-1783.

1. Alexander Macdonell (Aberchalder)—Captain 1st Battalion King's Royal Regiment of New York—8 years. (Had been an Aide-de-Camp to Prince Charles Stuart in 1745.)

2. Angus Macdonell—Captain 1st Battalion King's Royal Regiment of New York (Ensign in 60th Regiment 8th July, 1760; Lieutenant in same 27th December, 1770)—25 years.

3. Allan Macdonell (Collachie)—Captain 2nd Battalion 84th Royal Highland Emigrant Regiment; prisoner of war to the Americans (father of Nos. 9 and 17.)

4. John Macdonell (Younger of Aberchalder), Vide R.C.V. Regiment, No. 1—Captain Butler's Rangers—5 years and 10 months. (Entered the service at the commencement of the War as Ensign and was subsequently Lieutenant in 84th Royal Highland Emigrant Regiment—3 years and 2 months; afterwards Lieutenant-Colonel 2nd Battalion R.C.V. Regiment of Foot.) ·-

5. John Macdonell (of the family of Scothouse)—Captain 1st Battalion King's Royal Regiment of New York— 8 years. (Had previously been in the Spanish army and was "out" in 1745.)

6. Archibald Macdonell (of the family of Leek)—Captain 1st Battalion King's Royal Regiment of New York— 8 years (afterwards Lieutenant of the County of Stormont and Colonel Stormont Militia)—Vide War of 1812, No. 7.

7. James Macdonell—Captain 2nd Battalion King's Royal Regiment of New York—8 years.

8. Allan Macdonell (of the family of Leek)—Captain-Lieutenant 1st Battalion King's Royal Regiment of New York—8 years.

9 Alexander Macdonell (Younger of Collachie, whose father and mother were prisoners of war to the Americans) —First - Lieutenant Butler's Rangers. (Entered the service as a Cadet in the King's Royal Regiment of New York. Served also as Ensign in 84th Royal Highland Emigrants)—7 years. Vide War of 1812, No. 4.

10. Hugh Macdonell (son of Aberchalder), Vide R.C.V. Regiment, No. 2—Lieutenant 1st Battalion King's Royal Regiment of New York—7 years. Under date Chelsea College, 23rd June, 1804, Colonel Mathews, for many years Military Secretary to Sir Frederick Haldimand and Sir Guy Carleton (Lord Dorchester), wrote as follows to the Under Secretary of State for War concerning this officer and his relatives mentioned in this list:—

" * * * His father and uncle left Scotland with their families and considerable property a few years before the rebellion in America, with a view to establish themselves in that country, having for that purpose carried out a number of their dependants. They obtained a valuable grant of land from Sir John Johnson on the Mohawk River, in the settlement of which they had made considerable progress.

"When the rebellion broke out, they were the first to fly to arms on the part of Government, in which they and their adherents—not less than 200 men—took a most active and decided lead, leaving their families and property at the mercy of the rebels.

"I was at that time quartered at Niagara, and an eye witness of the gallant and successful exertions of the Macdonells and their dependants, by which, in a great measure, the Upper Country of Canada was preserved, for on this little body a very fine battalion was soon formed and afterwards a second."
[R. R. N. Y., 1st and 2nd Batt.]

"Captain Macdonell's father and uncle, at that time advanced in years, had companies in that corps, and in which his elder brother" (No. 4), "afterwards an active and distinguished partizan, carried arms. The sons of both families, five or six in number, the moment they could bear arms, followed the bright example of their fathers, and soon became active and useful officers in that and another corps of Rangers" (Butler's), "whose strength and services greatly contributed to unite the Indians of the Five Nations in the interest of Government, and thereby decidedly to save the Upper Country of Canada and our Indian trade."

11. Ranald Macdonell—Lieutenant 84th Regiment (Royal Highland Emigrants)—8 years and 4 months (formerly in 17th Regiment).

12. Archibald Macdonell—Lieutenant 84th Regiment (Royal Highland Emigrants)—(War of 1812, No. 8.)

13. Angus Macdonell—Lieutenant 74th Regiment.

14. Chichester Macdonell (son of Aberchalder)—2nd Lieutenant Butler's Rangers—6 years. (Afterwards commanded 82nd Regiment of Foot. Gold medal for Corunna. Died on service in India.)

15. Miles Macdonell (of the family of Scothouse)—Lieutenant 1st Battalion King's Royal Regiment of New York—2 years. (Afterwards Captain 2nd Battalion R.C.V. Regiment of Foot.)

16. Ranald Macdonell (of the family of Leek)—Lieutenant 2nd Battalion King's Royal Regiment of New York —3 years.

17. James Macdonell (son of No. 3)—Prisoner of war; subsequently Captain 43rd Light Infantry Regiment; died on service in West Indies.

ADVENT OF THE FIRST CATHOLIC PRIEST TO
UPPER CANADA (NOW ONTARIO) AS CHAPLAIN
TO THE HIGHLAND CATHOLIC U.E. LOYALISTS,
UNDER THE AUSPICES OF THE KING, 1785.

ADVENT OF THE FIRST CATHOLIC PRIEST TO UPPER CANADA (NOW ONTARIO) AS CHAPLAIN TO THE HIGHLAND CATHOLIC U.E. LOYALISTS, UNDER THE AUSPICES OF THE KING, 1785.

LORD HOBART, COLONIAL SECRETARY TO LIEUTENANT-GOVERNOR HAMILTON.

(Canadian Archives, Series Q, 24-2, p. 279.)

"WHITEHALL, 24th June, 1785.

"SIR,—Having laid before the King a Memorial of Mr. Roderick Macdonell, stating that, at the solicitation of a considerable number of Scots Highlanders and other British subjects of the Roman Catholic persuasion, who, prior to the last War, were inhabitants of the back settlements of the Province of New York, and to whom, in consideration of their loyalty and services, lands have been lately assigned in the higher parts of Canada, he is desirous of joining them in order to serve them in the capacity of a clergyman, in the humble hope that, on his arrival at their settlement, he shall be allowed by Government an annual subsistence for the discharge of that duty, I enclose to you the said Memorial, and am to signify to you the King's commands that you do permit Mr. Macdonell to join the above-mentioned settlers and officiate as their clergyman; and that with respect to the allowance to be made to him, I shall take an early opportunity of communicating to you His Majesty's pleasure.

"I am, etc.,

"SYDNEY."

[NOTE.—The Rev. Mr. Roderick Macdonell, of the family of Leek, was the brother of Captain Archibald Macdonell No. 6, Captain Allan Macdonell No. 8, and Lieut. Ranald Macdonell No. 16, Rev. War, and a relative of most of the other gentlemen mentioned in that list.]

ROYAL CANADIAN VOLUNTEER REGIMENT
OF FOOT.

ROYAL CANADIAN VOLUNTEER REGIMENT OF FOOT.

(REGULAR ESTABLISHMENT OF THE ARMY, 1796-1802.)

The first Regiment raised in Upper Canada (now the Province of Ontario).

2ND BATTALION R.C.V. REGIMENT OF FOOT.

Headquarters, Fort George.

Detachments at Fort Chippewa, Fort Erie, Amherstburg, Kingston and St. Joseph's Island.

[NOTE.—The 1st Battalion of this Regiment, under the command of Lieut.-Colonel the Baron de Longueuil, with Louis de Salaberry as Major, garrisoned the posts of the Province of Quebec.]

1. Lieut.-Col. John Macdonell (Aberchalder) — (No. 3, Rev. War)—served 15 years and 4 months: 3 years and 2 months late 84th Regiment; 5 years and 10 months late Butler's Rangers, and 6 years and 4 months R.C.V.—Colonel Commanding Glengarry Militia Regiment, 1803, and Lieutenant of the County of Glengarry. One of the two first members for Glengarry, 1792, and Speaker of the first House of Assembly of the Province of Upper Canada, now Ontario.

2. Hugh Macdonell (Aberchalder)—Captain (Rev. War, No. 10), subsequently Senior Captain 1st Battalion R.C.V.; Lieut.-Colonel Glengarry Militia Regiment, 1803. One of the two members for Glengarry in First House of Assembly, 1792. First Adjutant-General of Militia, Upper Canada; Assistant Commissary-General at Gibraltar, 1805 (Staff of H.R.H. the Duke of Kent); His Majesty's Consul-General at Algiers, 1811-20.

   "His Royal Highness" (the Duke of Kent) "has always understood from those who have had occasion to be acquainted with his proceedings at Algiers that his conduct has invariably met with the highest appreciation of Government for the judgment and firmness he has evinced in the most trying moments, a circumstance particularly gratifying to the Duke, who reflects with pleasure upon his being the first who brought him forward."—Extract from a letter written by Lieutenant-Colonel Harvey, by command of H.R.H. the Duke of Kent, at the time of Mr. Macdonell's death.

3 Miles Macdonell—Captain (Rev. War, No. 15); served 8 years: 2 years King's Royal Regiment of New York and 6 years in R.C.V. (afterwards Governor of Assiniboia in Lord Selkirk's Company).

4. Ranald Macdonell—Lieutenant; served 32 years and 7 months: 6 years and 6 months in 17th Regiment; 12 years in 60th Regiment; 8 years and 4 months in late 84th Regiment, and 5 years and 9 months in R.C.V.

5. Angus Macdonell—Lieutenant, 6 years.

NOTE.—The officers of this Battalion tendered their services "in any part of the globe to which they might have the honour to be called," and the men offered to extend their services as Fencibles throughout British America   These offers were acknowledged by H.R.H. the Duke of Kent as follows:—

Extract of letter from the Duke of Kent to Lieutenant-General Hunter, commanding the Forces in the Canadas, through his Aide-de-Camp, Major Gordon.

"Kensington Palace, December 15, 1800.

"With respect to your letter of the 26th of July, containing an enclosure from Lieutenant-Colonel Macdonell, commanding the Second Battalion Royal Canadian Volunteers, of the four companies of that corps, stationed at Kingston and Amherstburg, to extend their services as Fencibles throughout British America, I am commanded to desire that the thanks of His Royal Highness may be communicated to those four companies for this fresh mark of their zeal for the service and attachment and loyalty to their Sovereign."

Letter from H R.H. the Duke of Kent to Lieutenant-General Hunter:—

"Pavillion, Brightelmstone, October 25, 1800

"Sir,—I have the pleasure to acknowledge the receipt of your letter No. 12, dated York, July 25, which reached me, together with its several enclosures, on the 25th ult.

"Your letter of the 26th of July to Major Gordon, enclosing Lieutenant-Colonel Macdonell's report that four more companies of the Second Battalion of the Royal Canadian Volunteers had volunteered the extension of their services to the whole of British North America, having arrived at the same time, I am enabled to desire you to authorize that officer to express to the officers and men of those companies my thanks in the same manner as he was desired to do to those of the former four.

"EDWARD."

GLENGARRY FENCIBLE (BRITISH HIGHLAND) REGIMENT, 1795-1802.

GLENGARRY FENCIBLE (BRITISH HIGHLAND) REGIMENT, 1795-1802.

This regiment was not a Canadian corps, but was raised from his estates in Glengarry, in Scotland, by Alastair Ranaldson Macdonell, 15th Chief of Glengarry. The letter of service which issued authorized its being raised as a Catholic corps, being the first that was raised as such since the Reformation. It was embodied in 1795, and was stationed in Guernsey until 1798, when it proceeded to Ireland, where it served during the Rebellion.

Like all other Fencible corps, it was disbanded during the Peace of Amiens in 1802. Its association with Canada took place thereupon, and was so intimate and fruitful of result as to warrant its insertion in this list.

The following letter was addressed by Lord Hobart, then Secretary of State for the Colonies, to Lieut.-General Hunter, Lieutenant-Governor of Upper Canada:—

"DOWNING STREET, 1st March, 1803.

"SIR,—A body of Highlanders, mostly Macdonells, and partly disbanded soldiers of the Glengarry Fencible Regiment, with their families and immediate connections, are upon the point of quitting their present place of abode, with the design of following into Upper Canada some of their relations who have already established themselves in that Province.

"The merit and services of the regiment in which a proportion of these people have served give them strong claims to any mark of favour and consideration which can consistently be extended to them; and, with the encouragement usually afforded in the Province, they would, no doubt, prove as valuable settlers as their connections now residing in the district of Glengarry, of whose industry and general good conduct very favourable representations have been received here.

"Government has been apprized of the situation and disposition of the families before described by Mr. Mac-

27

donell, one of the ministers of their Church and formerly Chaplain to the Glengarry Regiment, who possesses considerable influence with the whole body. He has undertaken, in the event of their absolute determination to carry into execution their plan of departure, to embark with them and direct their course to Canada.

"In case of their arrival within your Government, I am commanded by His Majesty to authorize you to grant, in the usual manner, a tract of the unappropriated Crown lands in any part of the Province where they may wish to fix, in the proportion of twelve hundred acres to Mr. Macdonell and two hundred acres to every family he may introduce into the Colony.

"I have the honour to be, Sir,

"Your most obedient, honourable servant,

"HOBART."

Among the officers of the regiment were the following, in addition to Colonel Alastair Ranaldson Macdonell of Glengarry, by whom it was raised and who was the first Colonel Commanding:

[NOTE.—This is taken from the Army List of 1798, when the regiment was stationed in Ireland, Glengarry being in command of the Brigade and Colonel Donald Macdonald Colonel of the regiment, with Charles Maclean as Lieut.-Colonel.]

Major—Alexander Macdonell.
Captains—Ranald Macdonell.
        Archibald Macdonell.
Captain-Lieutenant and Captain—Alexander Macdonell.
Lieutenant—James Macdonell.
Ensigns—Alexander Macdonell.
       Donald Macdonell.
       Archibald Macdonell.
       Alexander Macdonell.
       Andrew Macdonell.
Adjutant—Donald Macdonell.
Chaplain—The Rev. Alexander Macdonell.
Quartermaster—Alexander Macdonell.
Surgeon—Alexander Macdonell.

COLONEL JOHN MACDONELL (ABERCHALDER)
OFFERS TO RAISE A REGIMENT OF
GLENGARRY HIGHLAND
FENCIBLES, 1807.

‵

COLONEL JOHN MACDONELL (ABERCHALDER) OFFERS TO RAISE A REGIMENT OF GLENGARRY HIGHLAND FENCIBLES, 1807.

COLONEL JOHN MACDONELL, LIEUTENANT OF THE COUNTY OF GLENGARRY, AND FORMERLY LIEUT.-COL. COMMANDING 2ND BATTALION R.C.V., TO COLONEL BROCK, COMMANDING IN UPPER CANADA.

"GLENGARRY, January 28th, 1807.

"SIR,—I have the honour to enclose you the proposals for raising a corps of Highland Fencibles in this County, which were submitted to your perusal. The alterations you made are adopted with very few exceptions: should they meet with your approbation, you will be pleased to forward them to the War Office.

"The permanent pay asked for the Field Officers and Chaplain may be considered unusual, but in this instance it is necessary and expedient for carrying the proposals into effect. The Field Officers must undergo a vast deal of trouble, and their time will be as much occupied as if the corps were constantly embodied.

"The County is almost entirely inhabited by Highlanders and their descendants, naturally brave and loyal as subjects, and firmly attached to the British Constitution and Government, yet from their situation and circumstances, being in general possessed of some landed property, and the high run of wages in the county, they are reluctant to quit these advantages to become soldiers. Nothing but a scheme of this nature, headed by gentlemen whom they know and respect, would induce them on any consideration to put themselves under the restraints of military discipline. The Chaplain having served in that capacity in the late Glengarry Fencibles in Great Britain, Ireland and Guernsey, has a claim to the favour of Government. He conducted a number of these people to this country, and having rendered himself useful in many respects to the people at large, has gained so far their confidence that his services in urging and forwarding this matter will be very essential. The adoption and successful issue of the present plan will greatly facilitate any future project of raising troops for a more general and extended nature of service.

"I have the honour to be, Sir,

"Your most obedient, humble servant,

"J. MACDONELL,

"Lieutenant of the County of Glengarry.

"Colonel Brock, &c."

COLONEL BROCK, COMMANDING IN UPPER CANADA, TO THE RIGHT HONOURABLE WILLIAM WYNDHAM, SECRETARY FOR WAR.

"QUEBEC, February 12, 1807.

"I have the honour to transmit for your consideration a proposal from Lieutenant-Colonel John Macdonell, late of the Royal Canadian Volunteers, for raising a corps among the Scotch settlers in the County of Glengarry, Upper Canada.

"When it is considered that both the Canadas furnish only 200 militia, who are trained to arms, the advantages to be derived from such an establishment must appear very evident.

"The militia force in this country is very small, and were it possible to collect it in time to oppose any serious attempt upon Quebec, the only tenable post, the number would of itself be insufficient to ensure a vigorous defence.

"This corps, being stationed on the confines of the Lower Province, would be always immediately and essentially useful in checking any seditious disposition, which the wavering sentiments of a large population in the Montreal district might at any time manifest In the event of invasion or other emergency, this force could be easily and expeditiously transported by water to Quebec.

"The extent of the country which these settlers occupy would make the permanent establishment of the staff, and one surgeon in each company, very advisable. I shall not presume to say how far the claims of the field officers to the same indulgence are reasonable and expedient.

"In regard to the Reverend Alexander Macdonell, I beg leave to observe that the men, being all Catholics, it may be deemed a prudent measure to appoint him Chaplain. His zeal and attachment to Government were strongly evinced while filling the office of Chaplain to the Glengarry Fencibles during the rebellion in Ireland, and were graciously acknowledged by His Royal Highness the Commander-in-Chief.

"His influence over the men is deservedly great, and I have every reason to believe that the corps, by his exertions, would be soon completed, and hereafter become a nursery from which the army might draw a number of hardy recruits.

"I have, &c.,

"Isaac Brock."

[Note.—Colonel Macdonell's suggestion was not immediately carried out. In 1812, upon the outbreak of war, the British Government practically adopted his plan, and the Glengarry Light Infantry Regiment was raised.]

RAISING OF THE GLENGARRY LIGHT INFANTRY REGIMENT FOR THE WAR OF 1812.

(REGULAR ESTABLISHMENT OF THE ARMY.)

COLONEL BAYNES, MILITARY SECRETARY TO LIEUT-GENERAL SIR GEORGE PREVOST, BART., COMMANDING IN CANADA, TO MAJOR-GENERAL BROCK.

"QUEBEC, December 12th, 1811.

"I am directed to transmit herewith a copy of proposals for raising a corps of Glengarry Fencibles. The Commander of the Forces has selected an officer of the King's Regiment, Captain George Macdonell, an avowed Catholic and a relative of the Glengarry priest of that name, to attempt the formation of a small battalion to be in the first instance under his command with the rank of Major, and in case a more respectable body can be collected, a Lieutenant-Colonel Commandant will be appointed. Captain Macdonell will leave this in a few days, and he will be directed to take an early opportunity of communicating with you as soon as he has felt his ground in Glengarry and is able to form a correct idea of the prospect and extent of success that is likely to attend his exertions."

COLONEL BAYNES, MILITARY SECRETARY TO LIEUT.-GENERAL SIR GEORGE PREVOST, BART., TO MAJOR-GENERAL BROCK.

"QUEBEC, May 14th, 1812.

"I have great satisfaction in telling you that I have reported the Glengarry Light Infantry more than complete to the establishment of four hundred rank and file, and have received Sir George Prevost's commands to recruit for a higher establishment—indeed, the quota the officers have engaged to fulfil will nearly amount to double that number, and from the very great success that has attended our exertions I have no doubt of succeeding by the end of the year. . "

WAR OF 1812-14.

WAR OF 1812-14.

MAJOR-GENERAL BROCK, PRESIDENT OF UPPER CANADA, TO THE LEGISLATURE OF THAT PROVINCE, 27th JULY, 1812.

"Honourable Gentlemen of the Legislative Council and Gentlemen of the House of Assembly.

"We are engaged in an awful and eventful contest. By unanimity and despatch in our councils and by vigour in our operations we will teach the enemy this lesson, that a country defended by free men, enthusiastically devoted to the cause of their King and Constitution, can never be conquered."

WAR OF 1812-14.

In this War the Men of Glengarry, the Glengarry Light Infantry Regiment and the Glengarry Militia, participated in the following Battles, Actions and Events:—

1. Capture of Detroit, August 16th, 1812.
2. Attack on Ogdensburg, October 4, 1812
3. Battle of Queenston Heights, October 12, 1812.
4. Engagement at St. Regis, October 23, 1812.
5. Capture of Fort Covington, November 23, 1812.
6. Capture of Ogdensburg, February 22, 1813.
7. Taking of York by Americans, April 27, 1813.
8. Battle of Fort George, May 27, 1813.
9. Attack on Sackett's Harbour, May 29, 1813.
10. Defence of Burlington Heights, July, 1813.
11. Battle of Chateauguay, October 26, 1813.
12. Skirmish at Hoople's Creek, November 10, 1813.
13. Raid from Cornwall on Madrid, February 6, 1814.
14. Capture of Oswego, May 6, 1814.
15. Battle of Niagara or Lundy's Lane, July 25, 1814.
16. Attack on Michilimacinac, August 14, 1814.
17. Attack on Fort Erie, August 15, 1814.
18. Second Battle of Fort Erie, September 17, 1814.
19. Skirmish at Lyon's Creek, October 19, 1814.
20. Expulsion of McArthur's Brigands, October 22, 1814.

WAR OF 1812-14.

1. John Macdonell (son of Greenfield) — Lieutenant-
   Colonel Militia; Aide-de-Camp and Military Secretary to Major-General Sir Isaac Brock, K.B. Nego-
   tiated on behalf of His Majesty's Force, the terms of
   the Capitulation of Fort Detroit by the Americans,
   August 16, 1812.

   Extract of despatch from Major-General Brock
   to His Excellency Sir George Prevost, Bart., Commanding in Canada, announcing the surrender of
   Detroit, dated Headquarters, Detroit, August 17,
   1812, published in a Gazette Extraordinary in
   London on 6th October:—

   "Brigadier-General Hull proposed a cessation of
   hostilities for the purpose of preparing terms of
   capitulation. Lieut.-Colonel Macdonell and Captain
   Glegg were accordingly despatched by me on this
   mission and returned within an hour with the con-
   ditions which I have the honour herewith to transmit.

   . . . .

   "I cannot on this occasion avoid mentioning the
   essential assistance I derived from John Macdonell,
   Esquire, His Majesty's Attorney-General, who, from
   the beginning of the War, has honoured me with his
   services as my Provincial Aide-de-Camp."

   [Gold Medal for the taking of Detroit; Killed at the Battle
   of Queenston Heights, October 12, 1812, æt. 27; Member
   for Glengarry, and Attorney-General of Upper Canada at the
   time of his death]

   "His Royal Highness has been pleased also to
   express his regret at the loss which the Province must
   experience in the death of the Attorney-General, Mr.
   Macdonell, whose zealous co-operation with Sir Isaac
   Brock will reflect lasting honour on his memory."

41

Extract of a despatch from the Right Honourable Earl Bathurst, K.G., one of His Majesty's principal Secretaries of State, to His Excellency Lieutenant-General Sir George Prevost, Bart., dated Downing Street, 8th December, 1812.

In communicating the above to Alexander Macdonell of Greenfield, the father of the Attorney-General, Lieutenant - Colonel Coffin, Provincial A.D.C., under date York, March 20th, 1813, stated by command of His Honour the President that "it would doubtless afford some satisfaction to all the members of the family of which the late Attorney-General was so great an ornament to learn that his merit has been recognized even by the Royal personage who wields the sceptre of the British Empire: on which His Honour commands me to declare his personal gratification."

2. Lieut.-Colonel George Richard John Macdonell ("Red George") — Lieut. Loyal British Fencibles, 1794; served in 55th Regiment in Holland, 1794; Lieutenant 8th Regiment, Captain 4th September, 1805; Major Glengarry Light Infantry Regiment, 6th February, 1812, which regiment was raised by him and the Reverend (afterwards the Hon. and Right Reverend) Alexander Macdonell; succeeded Colonel Pearson in command at Fort Wellington (Prescott), February 13th, 1812; appointed Inspecting Field Officer, vice Cotton, dec.; commanded at capture of Ogdensburg, February 13th, 1813 (wounded).

Letter from His Excellency Sir George Prevost, Commanding in Canada, to Lieut.-Colonel Macdonell:—

"KINGSTON, 24th February, 1813.

"MY DEAR SIR,—Although you have rather exceeded my orders, I am well pleased with what you have done, and so I have just told you in a General Order, which is to announce to the troops in British America your achievement.

"I am, yours faithfully,

"GEORGE PREVOST."

The General Order stated that . . . "His
Excellency feels much pleasure in publicly expressing
his entire approbation of the gallantry and judgment
with which the taking of Ogdensburg appears to have
been conducted. A salute to be fired immediately."

Thanks of the House of Assembly of Upper
Canada to Lieut.-Colonel Macdonell, 8th March,
1813, for "the splendid victory at Ogdensburg."

Second in command at Battle of Chateauguay;
Gold Medal; Bvt. Lt.-Colonel, 24th February, 1814;
C.B., 5th February, 1817 (for Ogdensburg and
Chateauguay); Lieut.-Colonel 79th Regiment.

3. The Reverend (afterwards the Honourable and Right
Reverend) Alexander Macdonell, formerly Chaplain
Glengarry Fencible (British Highland) Regiment; the
first Catholic Chaplain in the British Army and first
Catholic Bishop of Upper Canada; was largely in-
strumental in raising both the above regiments; appointed a member of the Legislative Assembly of
Upper Canada and awarded a pension of £800 per
annum by the British Government in recognition of
his services to the Crown.

4. The Hon. Alexander Macdonell (Collachie) (No. 9, Rev
War) — Colonel Militia and Deputy Paymaster-
General; made prisoner of war at capture of Niagara,
26th May, 1813; confined at Lancaster, Pennsyl-
vania, where his father had also been prisoner of war
during Revolutionary War; member for Glengarry
and Speaker House of Assembly, 1804; afterwards
member Leg. Council, U.C.

5. Duncan Macdonell (Greenfield)—Captain Flank Company 1st Regiment Glengarry Militia, 2nd January,
1809; Lieut.-Colonel 2nd Glengarry Militia, 1st
January, 1822; retired retaining rank, 3rd September, 1857, the Commander-in-Chief declaring, in
General Orders of that date, "his unwillingness to
permit this officer to retire from the command of this
battalion without recording the sense he entertains of
the value of his long and faithful service in the
Militia of the Province, dating from the last War."

6. Donald Macdonell (Greenfield)—Captain Flank Company 2nd Regiment Glengarry Militia, 15th April, 1812; Asst. Quartermaster-General Eastern District, 1813; Lieut.-Colonel Commanding same regiment, January 1, 1822; raised by instructions of Lieut.-General Sir John Colborne, K.C.B., Commanding in Canada (afterwards Lord Seaton), 15th January, 1838, and commanded Lancaster Regiment Glengarry Highlanders, which served in Lower Canada during the Rebellion; Deputy Adjutant-General Militia, U.C., 1846-61.

"MILITIA GENERAL ORDER.
"QUEBEC, 1st October, 1853.

"The Lieutenant-General, Administrator of the Government, being unavoidably prevented from attending the ceremony of depositing the remains of the lamented Major-General Sir Isaac Brock and his Aide-de-Camp, Lieutenant-Colonel Macdonell, and laying the corner stone of the monument about to be raised on Queenston Heights, has been pleased to appoint, as his representative on that deeply interesting occasion, Colonel Donald Macdonell, Deputy Adjutant-General of Militia for Canada West.

"His Excellency has much pleasure in nominating for this duty the brother of the gallant officer who fell nobly by the side of the Major-General in the performance of his duty as Provincial Aide-de-Camp.

"Lieutenant-Colonel De Salaberry, Deputy Adjutant-General, Canada East, and Lieutenant-Colonel Irvine, Provincial Aide-de-Camp, will be pleased to accompany Colonel Macdonell on this occasion."

7. Archibald Macdonell (Leek)—(Rev. War, No. 6)—Assistant Adjutant-General Eastern District; Lieut.-Colonel Stormont Militia and Lieutenant of the County of Stormont.

8. Archibald Macdonell (Rev. War, No. 12)—Lieut.-Colonel 1st Regiment Prince Edward Militia, 2nd January, 1800; Lieutenant of the County of Prince Edward.

. Alexander Macdonell-Greenfield (father of Nos. 1, 4, 5, r6
War of 1812)—Lieut.-Colonel 2nd Regiment Glengarry Militia.

. John Macdonell (of the family of Leek)—Lieut. Incorporated Militia Regiment; severely wounded at Battle of Niagara (Lundy's Lane); died of wounds at York, 15th August, 1814.

. John Macdonell (of the family of Leek)—Captain Flank Company 1st Regiment Dundas Militia, 25th December, 1812; wounded at capture of Ogdensburg, 22nd February, 1813; Captain Incorporated Regiment of Militia.

. Donald Macdonell—Lieut. 1st Regiment Stormont Militia, 7th January, 1809; died on service, 20th March, 1813.

Forbes Macdonell—Captain 10th Royal Veteran Battalion.

A. C. Macdonell—Ensign 104th (New Brunswick Regiment).

Ranald Macdonell — Lieutenant Canadian Fencible Regiment.

Alexander Macdonell—Captain 1st Regiment Glengarry Militia, 17th April, 1812—Ensign Glengarry Light Infantry Regiment, 8th October, 1812.

Angus Macdonell—Lieut. 2nd Regiment Glengarry Militia, 16th April, 1812; Ensign Glengarry Light Infantry Regiment, 6th February, 1812.

John Macdonell (son of No. 5, Rev. War)—Captain Canadian Corps of Voyageurs, 2nd October, 1812; formerly Ensign Cornwall Militia, 20th June, 1788; Lieut.-Colonel 1st Prescott Regiment, 1st April, 1822.

Donald Æneas Macdonell (son of No. 15, Rev. War, and No. 3, 2nd Battalion R.C.V.)—Gentleman Volunteer Glengarry Light Infantry Regiment; Ensign 8th (King's Royal) Regiment; severely wounded at Battle of Niagara (Lundy's Lane); afterwards Lieut Royal Tipperary Regiment (Vide Suppression Canadian Rebellion, No. 23).

20. James Macdonell—Gentleman Volunteer Nova Scotia Fencible Regiment, 24th August, 1814.

21. Donald Macdonell—Assistant Quartermaster Militia Midland District.

22. Alexander Macdonell—Ensign 2nd Regiment Glengarry Militia, 23rd April, 1812; Lieutenant 2nd Regiment Glengarry Militia, July, 1813.

23. Allan Macdonell—Ensign 2nd Regiment Glengarry Militia, 25th April, 1812.

24. John Macdonell—Captain 1st Regiment Stormont Militia.

25. Archibald Macdonell—Ensign 1st Regiment Stormont Militia, 2nd January, 1809.

26. James Macdonell—Quartermaster-Lieutenant 1st Regiment Dundas Militia, 29th January, 1813.

27. A. Macdonell—Ensign 1st Regiment Glengarry Militia.

28. James Macdonell—Lieutenant 1st Regiment Glengarry Militia, 2nd February, 1810; Captain 1st Regiment Glengarry Militia, 8th December, 1813.

29. Duncan Macdonald—Lieutenant Incorporated Militia Regiment.

30. Duncan Macdonell—Lieut. Flank Company 2nd Regiment Fencible Militia.

31. Allan Macdonell—Captain 1st Regiment Glengarry Militia.

32. James Macdonell—Ensign Flank Company 2nd Regiment Glengarry Militia, 22nd April, 1812.

33. Alexander Macdonell—Lieutenant 1st Regiment Glengarry Militia, 22nd February, 1812.

34. Peter Macdonell—Lieutenant 1st Regiment Glengarry Militia.

35. Alexander Macdonell—Quartermaster 2nd Regiment Glengarry Militia.

36. Alexander Macdonell—Ensign 2nd Regiment Glengarry Militia, Lieutenant 2nd Regiment Glengarry Militia, 25th January, 1814.

37. John Macdonell—Captain 2nd Glengarry Militia.

38. Donald Macdonell—Captain 2nd Glengarry Militia.

39. Angus Macdonell—Lieutenant 2nd Glengarry Militia; Captain, 12th April, 1812.

40. Allan Macdonell—Lieutenant 2nd Glengarry Militia; Captain, 13th July, 1812.

41. Alexander Macdonell — Lieutenant 2nd Glengarry Militia, 18th April, 1812.

42. Ranald Macdonell—Ensign 2nd Regiment Glengarry Militia, 22nd April, 1812.

43. Henry Macdonell—Captain 1st Regiment Prince Edward Militia, 24th March, 1813.

SUPPRESSION OF REBELLION, 1837-8.

"I beg to state that the county of Glengarry has on every occasion been distinguished for good conduct, and will on any emergency turn out more fighting men in proportion to its population than any other in Her Majesty's Dominions."

Extract from letter from Lieut.-Colonel Carmichael, Particular Service, to Lieut.-General Sir James Macdonell, K.C.B., K.C.H., commanding Brigade of Guards and second in command of Her Majesty's Forces in Canada, dated December, 1840.

SUPPRESSION OF REBELLION IN UPPER AND LOWER CANADA, 1837-38.

1. Sir James Macdonell (brother of Glengarry) — Lieutenant-General, K.C.B., K.C.H., commanding Brigade of Guards, and second in command of Her Majesty's Forces during the Rebellion; appointed a Member of Lord Durham's Special Council 28th June, 1838; Lieutenant-Colonel Coldstream Guards at Waterloo, where he defended Hougomont; Colonel 79th Highlanders, 14th July, 1842. Gold medal for Maida; Waterloo medal; medal and clasps for Salamanca, Vittoria, Nivelle and the Nive, Order of Maria Theresa and a Knight (4th class) of St. Vladimir, Principal Equerry to the Queen Dowager.

2. Donald Macdonell (of the family of Greenfield) (War of 1812, No. 6)—Raised by instructions of Lieutenant-General Sir John Colborne, K.C.B., commanding in Canada (dated 15th January, 1838), and commanded the Lancaster (2nd) Regiment of Glengarry Highlanders, which served in Lower Canada (at Napierville and Beauharnois), and subsequently in Upper Canada.

3. Duncan Macdonell (Greenfield) (War of 1812, No. 5)— Lieutenant-Colonel 2nd Regiment Glengarry Militia.

4. Alexander Macdonell (Aberchalder)—Major Lancaster (2nd) Regiment Glengarry Highlanders.

5. Donald Macdonell (Buidh)—Captain Lancaster (2nd) Regiment Glengarry Highlanders.

6. Alexander Macdonell (Lot No. 33, 6 con. Lancaster)— Ensign Lancaster (2nd) Regiment Glengarry Highlanders.

7. George Macdonell (of the family of Greenfield)—Captain Lancaster (2nd) Regiment Glengarry Highlanders.

8. Angus Macdonell—Lieutenant Lancaster (2nd) Regiment Glengarry Highlanders.

9. Alexander Macdonell (of the family of Greenfield)—Ensign Lancaster (2nd) Regiment Glengarry Highlanders.

10. Ranald Macdonell—Captain Lancaster (2nd) Regiment Glengarry Highlanders.

11. John Allan Macdonell (styled Agent)—Ensign Lancaster (2nd) Regiment Glengarry Highlanders.

12. Donald Macdonell—Captain 3rd (Lochiel) Regiment Glengarry Militia.

13. Donald Macdonell—Lieutenant (3rd) Lochiel Regiment Glengarry Militia.

14. A. Macdonell—Lieutenant 1st (Charlottenburgh) Regiment Glengarry Militia. (Commission dated January 1, 1838.)

15. A. Macdonell—Ensign 1st (Charlottenburgh) Regiment Glengarry Militia. (Commission dated January 1, 1838.)

16. Angus Macdonell—Colonel 4th (Kenyon) Regiment Glengarry Militia. (Commission dated June 27, 1837.)

17. A. Macdonell—Lieut.-Col. 4th (Kenyon) Regiment Glengarry Militia. (Commission dated October 18, 1837.)

18. A. Macdonell (Insh)—Major 4th (Kenyon) Regiment Glengarry Militia. (Commission dated October 18, 1837.)

19. G. Macdonell—Captain 4th (Kenyon) Regiment Glengarry Militia. (Commission dated October 18, 1837.)

20. Neil Macdonell (Surveyor Indian Lands)—Captain 4th (Kenyon) Regiment Glengarry Militia. (Commission dated October 19, 1837.)

21. A. Macdonell—Captain 4th (Kenyon) Regiment Glengarry Militia. (Commission dated October 20, 1837.)

22. A. Macdonell—Lieutenant 4th (Kenyon) Regiment Glengarry Militia. (Commission dated October 18, 1837.)

23. Donald Æneas Macdonell (of the family of Scothouse) (War of 1812, No. 19)—Lieutenant-Colonel Stormont Regiment of Militia; had served as a volunteer in the Glengarry Light Infantry Regiment during War of 1812-14, and was afterwards a Lieutenant in the 98th (Royal Tipperary) Regiment. Member for Stormont in several Parliaments and Warden Provincial Penitentiary, 1849-69.

24. J. Macdonell—Lieutenant-Colonel 1st Regiment Dundas Militia. (Commission dated April 29, 1837.)

25. J. Macdonell—Lieutenant-Colonel 2nd Regiment Dundas Militia. (Commission dated April 29, 1837.)

26. John Macdonell—Colonel Prescott Militia Regiment. (Commission dated April 1, 1822.)

27. A. Macdonell—Lieutenant-Colonel Russell Regiment Militia. (Commission dated January 4, 1838.)

28. A. Macdonell — Lieutenant - Colonel Northumberland Militia Regiment. (Commission dated January 5, 1838.)

29. A. Macdonell—Captain 1st Regiment Stormont Militia. (Commission dated January 14, 1822.)

30. R. Macdonell—Captain 1st Regiment Stormont Militia. (Commission dated May 26, 1835.)

31. A. Macdonell—Captain 1st Regiment Stormont Militia. (Commission dated February 1, 1838.)

32. R. Macdonell—Captain 1st Regiment Stormont Militia. (Commission dated February 1, 1838.)

33. J. Macdonell—Captain 1st Regiment Stormont Militia. (Commission dated December 26, 1838.)

34. A. Macdonell—Lieutenant 1st Regiment Stormont Militia. (Commission dated November 9, 1827.)

35. A. Macdonell—Lieutenant 1st Regiment Stormont Militia. (Commission dated February 1, 1838.)

36. D. Macdonell—Lieutenant 1st Regiment Stormont Militia. (Commission dated February 1, 1838.)

37. J. Macdonell—Ensign 1st Regiment Stormont Militia. (Commission dated November 13, 1827.)

38. A. Macdonell—Ensign 1st Regiment Stormont Militia. (Commission dated May 26, 1835.)

39. A. Macdonell—Ensign 1st Regiment Stormont Militia. (Commission dated February 1, 1838.)

40. Alexander Macdonell (of the family of Greenfield)— Captain Glengarry Light Infantry Company (stationed at Coteau du Lac). For many years Lieut.-Colonel Dundas Militia.

41. Reginald Macdonell (of the family of Greenfield)—Ensign Glengarry Light Infantry Company. On Staff Colonel C. B. Turner, K.H., Particular Service. Afterwards Lieutenant and Adjutant Royal Canadian Rifle Regiment until his death.

42. Æneas Macdonell (of the family of Greenfield)—Ensign Glengarry Light Infantry Company.

Lightning Source UK Ltd.
Milton Keynes UK
UKHW022318080223
416651UK00001B/40

9 781355 291077